Praise for John Macker:

"Veteran southwest poet John Macker has entered a habanero phase of writing where ocotillo blossoms *scorch what is left of (his) shadow*. His new book, *Atlas of Wolves*, is a night-goggle view of a badlands of the human heart where wolves are *blamed... for earth's dark capriciousness*. It opens with a genocidal *inventory of darkness* and closes with newly discovered universal matter's *inventory of light*. In between is an orison of concerns as topical as a border wall filled with narcocorridos and the bones of the deported, and as mystical as an invocation of the Rio Grande Gorge's *vibration of buried time*. Enigmas and elegies abound in *Atlas of Wolves*. Macker conjures past poets, such as Duncan, Spicer, Creeley, and Vallejo, musicians like Monk and Coleman, artists including Khalo and Motherwell, and departed souls of his family. He leads us on the trail of the vanishing jaguar, and he reminds us that the *tiny migrating hearts of hummingbirds beat within us.*"

-Donald Levering, Tor House Foundation
Robinson Jeffers Prize Winner and author
of *Coltrane's God* and *Previous Lives*

"Located at the intersection of the natural world and the imagination, these poems in *Atlas of Wolves* create a geography of their own. It is a place of integration, where geopolitical borders mean less than interconnection and wholeness. Inspired by the likes of Coyote, Robert Oppenheimer, and Vallejo, it is poet John Macker who creates this luminous vision, and invites us in."

-Miriam Sagan author of *Geographic: A Memoir of Time and Space*

"In *Atlas of Wolves*, John Macker's *inventory of darkness* is not only epic in scope but in its desire to examine mortality and immortality with an ever-changing lens of both cynicism and new-found wonderment. In an age where we desperately need a new breed of outlaw poetry, one needs to look no further than the ever-expanding work from this New Mexico master."

        -Lawrence Welsh, author of *Cutting the Wire* (with Ray Gonzales.)

"*Atlas of Wolves* is an incredibly strong work. His craft has grown in two directions – the poems in this volume are more foundational, placing deep roots in the lyrical earth. At the same time, his images have taken flight, becoming more vivid, original – at times they are truly startling and surreal. This is a great book, it has heft, depth and creative fire."

        -John Nizalowski, author of *East of Kayenta*.

Atlas of Wolves

Poems by John Macker

Stubborn Mule Press
Devil's Elbow, MO
stubbornmulepress.com

Copyright © John Macker, 2019
First Edition 1 3 5 7 9 10 8 6 4 2
ISBN: 978-1-950380-15-2
LCCN: 2019936696

Design, edits and layout: Jeanette Powers
Cover image: Annie Macker
Title page image: Annie Macker
Author photo: Annie Macker
All rights reserved. No part of this publication may be reproduced or transmitted in any form or by any means, electronic or mechanical, including photocopying, recording or by info retrieval system, without prior written permission from the author.

Many thanks to the editors of the following in print and on line publications where some of these poems, in present or previous versions, first appeared:

Malpais Review: "Thelonious Sphere Monk",
Chiron Review: "Crossing summer 2014",
"Elements of Mystery and Surprise."
Duke City Fix: "The Old Place, At the Anasazi Winery",
Mas Tequila "Solstice Walking Poem", "Coyote Journalist",
Sin Fronteras #20: "Leaving Notes for the Underworld",
Santa Fe Literary Review: On the Borderline with Pancho Villa",
Pinyon: "Saguaro",
Lummox Journal #5, Truck: "Massacre",
Café Review: "The Spicer Variations", "Paris Elegy #5",
Watermelon Isotope: "Standing Rock", "Indian Summer",
"Atlas of Wolves"
PoetsSpeak Anthology: Hers: "In Santiago's Hallway",
PoetsSpeak Anthology: Water: "Standing Rock",
"On the Day They Polluted the Animas River",
Mortar Magazine: "Still Life with Border Crossers",
Manzano Mountain Review: "Birds",
Grand Junction (Colorado) Sentinel: "Birds of the Gulf Coast",
Pilgrimage: "Indian Summer"
PoetsSpeak Anthology: Walls: "On the Borderline with Pancho Villa",
"Navigating an Archipelago of Treacheries"
Turtle Island Quarterly: "The Longest Night",
Miriam's Well (blog): "Elements of Mystery and Surprise."
Lummox Journal #7, Fungi: "Anthropocene."
Missing Persons: "Aeolian."
Montrose Mirror: "At the Anasazi Winery."
Black Ace/Long Road postcard poem: "Gila."
Gasconade Review/Gas Station Famous: "Border Wall Blues,"
"Buried Poem", "Empty Foxhole", "Lenitive."

An excerpt from the poem, "On the Day They Polluted the Animas" appeared in *Wilderness: land untrammeled* exhibit at the Page Coleman Gallery in Albuquerque, NM & chapbook, published by Collective Perception. Special thanks to Dale Harris.

The following poems appeared in *Gorge Songs,* 8 limited edition folios featuring 12 poems and original woodblock art by Leon Loughridge, (Denver: DCArt Press, 2017/18): "Gorge Song", "Poem/river", "St. Patrick's Day", "Rio Grande Gorge: in memorium", "Turning for Home," "The River", "September", "Robert Creeley in Taos", "Solstice River Poem", "The River's End", "Christmas at Picuris Pueblo", "Solstice Walking Poem".

Special thanks to John Nizalowski, Miriam Sagan, Jeanette Powers, Donald Levering, Lawrence Welsh and Jason Ryberg.

Atlas of Wolves

CONTENTS

Still Life with Border Crossers

On the Borderline with Pancho Villa / 1

Still Life with Border Crossers / 2

El Linea / 8

Border Wall Blues / 9

Outlaws of the Greenest Planet / 12

Navigating an Archipelago of Treacheries / 14

Incident at Tinaja del Indio / 16

At the Anasazi Winery / 19

Birds / 20

Birds of the Gulf Coast / 22

Saguaro / 23

Atlas of Wolves / 24

The Longest Night / 29

Winter Poem / 30

Buried Poem / 32

In Santiago's Hallway / 34

Thelonius Sphere Monk / 35

Empty Foxhole / 37

"the wind is in charge of lives tonight" / 38

To My Mother / 39

Book of Wind / 41

Aeolian / 43

Lamentation of J. Robert Oppenheimer / 44

The Spicer Variations / 46

Coyote Journalist / 48

Massacre / 50

Paris Elegy #5 / 52

Paris Elegy #6 / 53

Elements of Mystery and Surprise / 55

In Praise of Winter's Essentials

Anthropocene / 58

First Day of Autumn / 60

Standing Rock / 61

Indian Summer / 62

In Praise of Winter's Essentials / 63

Poem to My Younger Self / 65

Distance Over Snow / 60

Late April / 70

Leaving Notes for the Underworld / 71

Lenitive / 72

Burial Ground / 74

the old place / 75

Moon Song / 76

Thankful / 77

Universe of Poems and Dreams / 79

Lone Essentials / 80

Gorge Songs

poem/river / 83

The River's End / 84

The Day They Polluted the Animas / 85

Gorge Song / 86

St. Patrick's Day / 87

Rio Grande Gorge: in memorium / 88

Turning for Home / 89

The River / 90

Robert Creeley in Taos / 92

September / 93

Solstice River Poem / 94

Christmas at Picuris Pueblo / 95

solstice walking poem / 96

This book is dedicated to
Robert P. Anderson Jr.
1954-2016
my friend

I

Still Life with Border Crossers

On the Borderline with Pancho Villa

for Lawrence Welsh

My famous river's edge
   cottonwoods
over one-hundred years old
are almost skeletons now
brittle deep roots in the worn hallowed ground
quenched by the medicine
of time's passage.
This is where our borders come
to pray against prayer
to grieve against grief

We're close enough to touch the
tragedy of Mexico
with our ghost fingers,
ascendant moon illuminates this ancient
fabric of space,
where the last revolution's
blue heron lifted off the Rio Grande
and once the smoke cleared:

where the blood reached deep ground
towards a new inventory of darkness.

Still Life with Border Crossers
After Vallejo

I.

Mayans called Mexican Jaguar
god of the underworld
is stopped cold in his tracks by
Arizona's border wall
followed by his shadow
followed by his ghost. His spot
patterns conjure images of butterflies.
Overhead, the Lyrids are a flock of
falling tears set aflame by their collision
                with an unsuspecting earth.

II.

Coyote laps last feeble inch
    of water from a mud puddle in

gran apacheria

eyes aglow with setting Orion
a paw print is a haiku
a brooding measure of belonging

a mandala

with a keen sense
of direction

starlight is the desert's muse.

III.

Dry-gulched by fate,
its man in black circled you for months.
To them you weren't human,
you were a border effigy
not even the sum total of your tracks
they discovered you sheltered in place.
News of your passing
was picked up in the borderlands
    and wired to April sky.
You are buried john doe
where the desert sun sears
pauper's graves
deep into the black folds of the earth.

IV.

The wind rode in side-saddle and in pieces

I had limbs of smoke

the dead air climbed up my arms

I rode memory into the ground

The turkey vultures circle in invisible cursives

above the wall   above the

the grace of the unfurled world

some days I

suffer from the velocity of moving without hope

under border wire . . .

V.

Sonoran Book of the Dead

Crossed it at all hours
listening to Black Sabbath or later,

the Miles of *Time After Time*
the desert of my youth

an apotheosis moonlit with
subversive promise

a twilight flotilla of yucca blossom
Buddha clouds harried by the wind

into a batch by nightfall. Before
memory became a book of the dead:

it all seemed to make sense because
it seemed to make sense of us.

A dollop of snow on the ocotillo
the secretive allure of vanquished light.

VI

Crossing summer 2014

The children are children of crossers
spit upon
called by other names
provokes the patriotic
howl of outrage
the sighing buses
mirror shades for windows
the border's blue silence draws
the desert exhausted
to a close.

Like Lorca's pomegranate
broken open in the heat:

the blood of the wounded earth
flows here

can be seen from unmarked
graves or
a vulture's perspective
but no substitute for the ice in
some *tejas* politician's clogged veins.

They say we are better armed
than the children
our drones are butterflies
with omnivorous eyes that watch us
during drought years
walk across the river
with our kids.

VII

imaginary effigy

they populate the borderlands
as warnings or
half-naked ghoulish trinkets
from a god dying of thirst.
As raggedy scarecrow children held up by
branches and twigs.
On hillsides and culverts.
They wear the condemned clothing found
cast off by the wilderness trekkers.
The Steller's jay is a nursery rhyme.

Their rhythmic
breathing is exiled to the
floor of creosote blossoms.
The ocotillo sway like the converted atop
a holy mountain.

El Linea

If I travel a bit farther north I'll find
my own grave, unmarked
                            full of holes from target practice
the adust end of the line.
In the end, the desert will consume me like a
    dry gaping failed Eden
an Agnes Martin landscape.
I lose my breath to the heat.   I thread
my way through the dense ocotillo, each
    blossom aflame
                    each one scorches what is left of my shadow.

I bleed incessantly, nothing closes my wounds.
My bones drop to the ground helter-skelter from no known heaven.
Thorn pricks, stigmatas, bullet creases   I wake
    in the Sonoran morning saddle-stitched by the sun and
the land once *sin fronteras* begs for no mercy.
These ghost rains of virga fall in rigid strands
            whispering from barely a cloud.

El Linea is masculine, knows no borders, accepts no grief,
    no beating heart, my mother was its slave.

The line belongs   the scourge of the invisible
tattooed on us all.

Border Wall Blues

When not speaking in tongues
its soullessness borders on the devout.
From the top of the wall, we're out of range
of anything animated or proselytizing
from the top of the wall
there are no degrees of separation
from the heat
the desert is a fever dreamt graveyard and
the wind is alive with hymns.
The wall wages a war of insurrection
on the landscape
dispossessed javelina mothers cry at the moon
rattlesnakes sell death rattles
safe for children without homes.

From up here, *el norte* loses its cool
but you can watch Jesus cross the Rio Grande
his flotation device a crown of thorns.
Mourning wolves' claws are styluses at play
in the furrows of the earth
evolution will one day take their sight
because of the impenetrable sameness of the night.
El linea is a lit fuse blessed by Saint Anthony
red dirt (marijuana) knocks on the door
of wall and is asked for its credentials
the view from the wall is commensurate with
    my capacity for wonder.

From the top of the wall
a couple of gringo poets under the spell
of some ebullient *anejo,*
talk surfing, confederate generals and
their capacity for wonder borders on the devout.
From the top of the wall you can see Zapata's horse
ride into the tequila sunrise and
pose for Diego Rivera's mural
while the sky shelters its rainbows from the dull light of day.
Wall's famous shadow is a military asset, is
impetuous and waits for nobody.

You can watch the children play cat's cradle
in the arroyo bottoms and learn to flirt
with the paranoia of barbed wire.

You can fill this hollow wall with the blues,
narcocorridos, the deported, the disappeared
our confederate generals
the bones of turkey vultures
splinters of our national cartilage
this is how we give solace to the underworld.

From here the crossers can see America's rapacious
crumbling beauty. Its army of oxidized statuary
in the moodiest of public parks reimagines war.
From the top of the wall the winds
drift down to Mexico and emboldened heat

they blow the untrammeled dust of crossers
until they've extinguished all fires.
This part of the wall is hell bent for heaven
because heaven invented speaking in tongues.
This part of the wall is dedicated to wooly
mammoths who once claimed all of Aztlán
as home, who respected no borders, whose
ghost migrations still leave deep tracks.
To the Rufous hummers who've been around as
long as the jawbone of an ass, who spend
twenty percent of their waking moments
in combat, who fly south every year
and obey the instinct that says one day
this ground will be made whole.

From the top of your lungs you can sing
                the partially eclipsed, white nationalist
                              grindhouse grievous angel blues.

Outlaws of the Greenest Planet

Out here, there's a dreamy, snake-
trance southern-fried dada quality to time
& space
        her hair, the color of nine-year old sour
mash, in a neurotic cascade of a braid
flowing
   down the small of her back
is pearl'd with sweat.

Sonoran border ranch motion sensor
camera takes a photo of a northern jaguar, he moves
with the unrepentant romance of
the endangered, the
drought so prolonged
               he doesn't leave tracks.

Listen to her string out a series of
loud *caws*
        each one replenishes itself   each
one reanimates the near distance.

I listen for my breathing to tame itself
I've abandoned my saints to the molten air but
there's an anecdotal sweetness
   to the red cardinal's spring tweets.

A mating pair of scorpions scratch an
    indecipherable language on the desert floor.

We've joined the outlaws of the greenest planet
the soft glancing blows of the past
the projectile mercilessness of the future
the sundry pollutions
                      all the shortened stays.

Navigating an Archipelago of Treacheries

Poppies are electric orange and bright as the sun. Wild roses climb up the wall into the sky. They bunch together in a refuge of fake, fallen stars that rustle restlessly in the May breeze. It is summer somewhere south of here. I can feel it coming, its wild breath in my face, warming without reassurance, on its trek from the borderlands to the high country.

Over the desert, past the shimmering hypnotic waves of bluish heat, into the mutated distance where the bad gods burned the border's razor sharp indivisibility into the unforgiving ground and fooled the eyes into thinking there was a shallow reservoir of water or at least to the heat crazy mind, a place that offered a provocatively safe, if not totally hallucinated respite from the clawing sun.

In Mexico journalists are disappearing like virga, no trace of their words touching ground. Where sacrifice has become bloody ritual, where each daily breath is caught in the act of gasping for prayer. Overheated silence replaces the words and the pages are worn by the wind into shreds, emptied of all meaning and the killing continues.

Border trekkers navigate an archipelago of treacheries and burnt-out days without succor or shade. They are accompanied by a corona of hummingbirds. They can hear the desert age, die and then renew itself in the rhetorical flourishes of songbirds. In the ascetic ramblings of the vinegaroon. The scent of it, at this moment, is shamelessly spring blossom sweet. We are coming for them but they are not waiting for us. We will freeze them in their tracks at the wall that somebody around here with circumspect knowledge of the issue is going to pay for. We will stop them in their paw prints. We will plunder animal and plant families and separate them from themselves. The coming heat and the purity of our mission will be relentless and without remorse.

Incident at Tinaja del Indio

In 1963, a group of California ornithologists visited Tinaja del Indio, basically a watering hole, in the Sierra Pinacate, a protected volcanic biosphere in Northern Sonora, Mexico. This tinaja was located on a hummingbird migration flyway and "the birds were as thick as honey bees at these watering holes and in dense vegetation of that wet year." This group of scientists managed to kill literally hundreds of the birds, "in the interest of science", and this exterminated the migratory flyway population and almost no hummers have been seen there since.

I.

In the spirit of silence
in the interest of science
out in that fragrant nectar corridor
above pumice earth
when we were all young and would live
forever, who had to kill us to dissect the

secrets of our youthful beauty?
Who spread our feathers out into dwarf
massacred headdresses to find our
diminished heartbeats in the blackened
volcanic heat?

Knowledge is power one of them said,
tamping sweet tobacco into his irritably tooth-pocked pipe.

No rites of separation,
not bound by empathy or *ahimsa*
no eulogies uttered by pesticide cowboys
in suburban dashboard Jesus trucks,
each corpse was pure flame at rest.
Most of the spirits of the dead had entered

bardo,
        the place only summer deserts understand.

II.

The perfume of extinction never reached this far north
but drifted like smoke from
the coyote bottom of the
planet back into Indian time.
In the yard, in nectar obsessed
congeries, their bold colors intimate

certain transient passions
that betray a complete deficit of tribal spirit:
hyper-alert in the lilac dripping with dew
like desperados waiting for a train.
This morning, I imagine the lone scout
arrived from South America

the perilous trek runs through his bloodstream
a river on fire. His feathers gleam burnished by first light.

He grooms himself with a tiny Samurai sword
beak perched on a branch the circumference
of a cello string. Every Autumn mourns when
they take their improvisational beauty with them.

They dare us to intuit their itinerary
First do no harm. Lastly, do no harm.
We are not harmless. I've been there, though,
where the flyway used to be, over that
uninhabited scorched earth's cratered space
where we conjure the tiny migrating hearts of
Mexico   no harm done   I must remember,

they beat within us.

At the Anasazi Winery

As Sherwin Bitsui read:

as they scrape double-plumed
birdsongs from the beaks of drowned
hummingbirds

a hummingbird enters
flits about the poet's head
perches on an orange extension cord
in the winery eaves and
then leaves
darting into the open
desert sky

a colorful word or two in its beak
the rest remain
invisible
floating in the dry air
seduced by his voice   we
tried to capture most of them
keep them close in the soft
cages of our minds

until no longer rarified or endangered,
until they've written themselves out
become birdsong

free to leave of their own accord.

Birds
—to Annie

In the wildlife refuge
a flock of snow geese ascends as one
loosely woven textile undulating in
the wind, white as a parliament of moons,
its light as a feather sojourn
in the shapelessness of time's passage
a contemplation of pure organic form.
It is nineteen degrees
January is one snowfall away from
lasting until spring.

A hobbled Jim Harrison died at his writing
table in his writing shack
finished but never finished
one of those presences
no beginning or end
one-eyed smash-mouthed angel
writing:
> *birds are poems I haven't caught yet*

Last words must defy gravity.

Some days winter is in name only. Some
days the wind chill is bone deep.
No lapses in wonder,
just the earth, indelicate caregiver,

accessorizing itself with
tapirs and titmice
lone pine tip thrasher's morning song
nuances that subvert power
spasms of uplift like this unfurling
snowscape of take your breath away birds.

–January 20, 2017

Birds of the Gulf Coast

In the eye of the storm
the air is as still as troubled sleep and
emptied of time. For the birds of Texas
or Louisiana, no mass migrations or
extinctions on the horizon, just those who
lost all sense of direction swimming through
oceans of air, who'll tell the kingfisher's god
all is forgiven even though it was us who invented
forgiveness. Who built downriver from the refineries and
superfund sites, who gave the Brazos its
untamed name, who can increase in intensity
or not, the monotony of the sun. Who think
birds will be the first to herald the Second Coming.
After days of lacerating rain veils, the myths,
rescued dogs, children and floating graves are
reconstituted into nuclear families, Hemingway's
house and the fifty-four six-toed cats survived intact,
the moon is a gentleman caller,
the rose petal clouds left behind are
strewn across its freshened light's path.

Saguaro

How many times did you whisper to James Wright: I *am* one of the gods? Some days when the past wintered over in my heart you gathered me in your arms and the flowing grace of your ground. Even the years you couldn't needle the sky for a glancing blow of endangered rain, I felt sheltered from the bitterest of Americas. Roadrunner circles you like Europa circles Jupiter, the inferno of June rattler coils around the bottom of your soul for warmth, elf owl nests in your low-rent flesh. Loss of habitat expands the grievous distance between gods, while during times of war, you stand sentinel, still, like the sphinx, arms frozen, lesson in sentience. You've survived Mark Klett's black and white photographs of you in ruins: longest day, last light of solstice, hollowed out, black as charcoal, collapsed by time, bullet-ridden, skyscrapers without a prayer, beyond repair, while off in the distance

> rattlesnake traverses
> a tire track in the noir dusk
> evening's aflame.

Atlas of Wolves

> *I keep dreaming I'm dead*
> *I keep feeling like I'm home.*
>
> —a wolf song of the Tlingit

I.

Somewhere around here
in the corpse mouth twilight,
they hog tied you   trapped you   muzzled you
filled you full of poison, bullets,
dragged you behind horses and wagons
               blamed you for earth's
dark capriciousness, for scoring one rattlesnake
and a roped goat. You scent-marked trails,
killed caribou, chased ravens, gave birth, grew old,
watched snow blanket your mate for life, in death.
It seemed only yesterday
you brought down camels in Oklahoma.
Instead of water, you draw bone-dead breezes from
wells of antipathy and they follow like acolytes.

Just as Modigliani nudes were once considered
pornography, you once ate the earth and
gobbled the children, crown prince of
pestilence in our dreams.

On the border,   *el lobo*
      patron saint of the incorrigibles,
        three hundred of you left in captivity.

They can't not stalk you, if they let you be
you'll just liberate them.
No one prays to the mournful ecstasy
of your song anymore.

Tonight, black swan sky swells under the stars
down below you survey the ruins
of Tsankawi in the eveningfall heat.
Nothing or no one is omitted.
Your paw print's remains in dried mud must be
a dream catcher, a sand painting
something besides your eyes
to see ourselves through.

II.

When you came to my house that day
you were mostly pure blooded
you dragged in the rust of sunsets
accusatory drought winds
your blissfully
untamed birds,
what on earth the world doing to itself
was rooted deep behind your eyes.
Barbed wire twisted in your fur.
Only in the deep star forest of a silent night
did you feel safe. You chased rings of
dust around my dogs. You gave charms

to my wife
                as the arroyos dried in July you
turned her into rain.

You waited until I was old enough
had enough poems in me to disinherit
a morsel of civilization for this bedeviled
ground. You would have protected us
with all of your lives. Your
                        el lobo life
your wretched outcast myth that only
stalks children at night, your
slathering border fallen angel
in the threatened deep wilderness of dreams,
                        lives.

III.

Shrunken habitat allows you to feel the
magnanimous heartbeat of the universe.
You posed for a plein air still life with border crossers.
You howled until the Buddha emptied your voice of fear.
On the San Augustin plain star clusters held their
breaths while you crossed in peace.
You crossed before a Mojave rattler that followed
you in medieval silence with its tongue.
You crossed the Caldera leaving
no tracks, no trace, no seeds.

You trekked across the parsimonious desert just as
Jesus Christ hallucinated Lucifer in another dimension.
On the Pakistan-Afghan border each lone sojourner's
howl is a seed planted by war torn feral blackened
night to insure the survival of your species as pure song.
You crossed your paws and left a mandala in the snow.
You cross paths with your ancestors so they won't take
solace in a future of musty museum dioramas.
Under a New York City Eucharist moon Miles Davis opens a
window and hears the most mournful *Summertime* in history.

IV.

Gila
      With a line by Ghassan Zaqtan

Traces of fresh snow on dry bark.
Low wooded hills blanket wrapped in
forgotten Apache answer the northern flicker's
staccato deadfall pecking with no language.
Brittle cold rattles the prayer stick thin
cottonwoods. Unrepentant paw prints in their
solitude say
        there is no hardship on a path leveled by wolves.

We follow tracks with our pharmaceuticals
and hair triggers

                  acknowledge the root word for
utopia in Greek means *no place.*

The Gila river courses down through the ponderosas
scratching for roseate desert, it embraces
every one of her senses with undiluted spiritual vigor.
This is the place where loba brings her children,
                  this is where she comes to clear her name.

Swallows work their spontaneous magic on the river
with the seasoned empathy of angels. She suffers an
embroidery of purgatories, can still see the ice age
moon's reflection on the surface.
She bends over the current for another drink
for this moment there are no conspiracies
no hardships
                  there's no place like home.

The Longest Night

Watching winter come in from the window
a tree has grown 30 feet at the spot where ashes
were buried long ago. In the near distance,
some of them are bare and barely there. Tonight
is the longest night of the year. The stinking
sumac looks like a menorah, the tip of each branch aflame
in the sunlight, each flame a dim after dark glow. There are

salt flats in Bolivia that turn into a mirror that reflects the sky
during the rainy season. It's called the border between heaven
and earth. Moisture is bare and barely there.
Tonight is the longest night of the year. Every night in the
diaspora is the longest, they pray to an earth that will either
swallow them whole or light their way. Beneath the ashes,
the old wounds travel underground. Tendrils of smoke rise
from each branch, the sky is deep enough to consume any flame.

Everyone remembers Jesus was born in the Middle East
and enjoyed the climate. The Star of Bethlehem glitters
between heaven and earth, is a Neil Young song,
it softens the hardened long night of the heart.

winter poem
After John Weiners

Driving through winter fog
it's difficult to see
a raven peck at the lost movie
in a coyote's
frozen eye
that last saw the morning
star, a hawk
kiting, an anxious flock of
cedar waxwings
or the world's wounds
tombs or bombs

Chinese Buddhist ceremonies
for the dead:
priests beckon vultures to feast on
the corpse,
then lift off the earth
with its spirit

transition should be regeneration

like crossing the border
like jazz /
        blues fusion

like old friends notifying
the earth they're pulling up stakes, just
a short winter's day away from night
or Seamus Heaney's last text
from his deathbed in Latin:
                noli timere

be not afraid!

Some mornings
it's hard to see your life in front
of your eyes
through this dusting of
desert snow
it was a good morning
to die
a myth   a feast.

Buried Poem

After Sam Shepard

The last motel room standing
with its million neon eyes
mad drunks and samurai crucifixions
died last night in Barstow
and Truth or Consequences, or Baggs, Wyoming.

Where we tore each other up in the dark and
reassembled ourselves, there were words for that.

There were words for the silences
and inflamed heirlooms, the migrations
our fathers left us —
endless abandoned blue streaks
of *that was the whisky talking* until the words
dried up emptied of all but their machismo.

There were words for motels like morose
wickiups where the past tongue-lashed
memory for failure to forgive after
all these years.

Room service stalked you
across the desert like a serial killer!
We watched you in that *Cold in July* flick,
Your character as taciturn as a tombstone.

What dystopia in human form
looked like ground to a pulp.

You made us famous for our trespasses,
our outlaw mouths,
our incendiary family arrhythmias.
There were words for every cutthroat summer
for every middle distance
as American as wide open space that disappears
while a river cleaves its fatally untamed ground.

In Santiago's Hallway*

La Llorona searches nightly forever
for her two drowned children
her long black hair glistens like death's
waterfall under border lights.
Pale faced and riven with guilt,
she haunts the river
scans obits freshened with war
returns to the shrine of Santiago's hallway
where she's honored as
                monstrous
                    beautiful
                        post-modern
                              black lit with *duende*
weeping mother
temptress, love sick killer
skeletal Madonna / whore of the desert

as fixated on death as a skull.
 Santiago holds the skull cane
he conjures her many meanings in his life
he can feel her eternal presence
he implores El Paso to return her
children from their watery graves.

She still breaches the wind
with infamous bereaved wails.

Narrow hallway as mini-art gallery at The Rock House, café & gallery, El Paso, TX., featuring numerous artistic renderings or interpretations of the long-dead mother, mythical La Llorona, who haunts the borderlands to this day, grieving loudly for the children.

Thelonious Sphere Monk

Straight no chaser of a highway
miles receding as if something cast a spell on them
like scaling the years one rung at a time
driving towards the grey of far rain Mexico
looking for a side canyon
some *rincon* where the improvised music
of water dripping like honey
        from a canyon ledge spring
or a canyon wren's lush
              singing
can be heard

where this dust devil of a woman's
desire is no lasting apparition
where banished echoes dance like there's
no exit   where
climate change drunk dials the earth.
           Let's sleep with all of them in the bottom
of the desert underneath stars as quiet as
day of the dead skulls and
dream Monk's dream
           dream Monk's dream!
leave the fire
wander around
twirl three times
return to its blue warmth
improvisation begats improvisation

because the night
is as mercurial as the god
who whispered an ancient universe
of secrets into
Thelonious Monk's ear.

Empty Foxhole

Ornette Coleman's death is the shape
of death's to come. He played the
breathless language of improvisational
blues and jazz until I could feel the world
embrace his overheated romantic madness.
It filled every foxhole with uninterrupted prayer.
Listening to Ornette I felt his sacred heart
blues, his squash blossom blues, his darkened
street blues. Listening to Ornette, he could rub his hands
together like a shaman's and create sparks.
Listening to Ornette is to hush the earth
blazing with war songs. Listening to Ornette
the summer heat seeks my bones
disappeared cities no longer spark the horizon.
His, the soul end of endings, the
lone gunman of ecstatic blow.

the wind is in charge of lives tonight
- Bob Kaufman

In San Francisco
jazz used to enter rooms
without knocking and fill every coffee
cup with free wine.

Every photo of him on the street,
wearing his vow
of silence like an umbrella,
is an epiphany
every furrow on his mugshot
face a confession
or a line of improvisatory music drawn in the sand.
Bob listens to jazz for the divinity of its sound.
Bob empties gurus of their self-knowledge
and lets them dance to his jazz poems.

Every time I listen to jazz
I know who is in charge of lives tonight.

To My Mother

I could almost feel your presence today
one quieted moment after another
not quite your voice, not quite the wind
in this cold rawness,
the confectionary snow
I wondered if they were your
whispers, disassembled and
from high beyond winter's reach
of the sky.

   Sometimes it's just a familiar river I hear —
am I my own best counsel for the
years remaining suspended in the future
riding on rapids, hostages of velocity until they reach
calm water warmed by a secret stillness?

   Sometimes it's the night as dark as
the devil's ass blackened by smoke
your harshest critic, each one darker than the last
took your breath in measured beats softly away.

   Sometimes it's the sky
with its fulgent stars, not so much a reckoning
of your presence in deep space as the
distant ruins of a familiarity I've invented
new ways to preserve.

The vague emptiness of the half feral ground
blessed by your foreshortened stay,
I walk across for miles in my mind.

Sometimes I can feel the empty chambers
of loss in our once shared memory.
Sometimes it is just the wind.

Book of Wind

She didn't live long enough
   to become a cailleach
that old Irish hag
        she died after
giving birth to my mother in winter

suddenly
    all the lingering cold snaps
all the wide open graces of wilderness
were drained from the air
   that we lost her
those frozen moaning winds of Wyoming told
us nothing
      few people were tenacious enough to
         establish roots there   but five young
daughters and my grandfather remained behind

tethered to her ground   all I know
is Anna came from mythic stone   she
   herded deer, her staff froze the earth   from
her Cliffs of Moher to the
   Isle of Man

the mystery brings me to life   my heart
must reassemble some things about her:

    she left few footprints   it was as
        if winter was where she came from   and
to winter returned.
        She still grieves over her
unborn daughter's death
from drink so many years away.
Their names join all the others
etched in the Book of Wind.

Aeolian

He asked me if I held him responsible
for my mother's slow descent into nothingness

all those years ago. He gripped the deck railing
memory had misplaced its herding instincts but

the summer heat filled his bones with light. His rice
paper skin, his white hair game show host perfect.

Telephone wires above us murmured like harp strings.
To my father, the blue sky out here was the sweltering Pacific,

war seen from underneath the ocean, a still breathing thing,
    Leyte Bay.
I asked myself, at this age, the currents of rivers so much

swifter than before, clots of shore ice breaking off &
floating rapidly towards some endless summer, was truth more

important than beauty? I answered him:
                          Of course not.

All recriminations silenced is the beauty of spring's first scented
rain, a loved one's inevitable absence leaving every darkened
    door ajar.

A poem heard only when recited by the wind.

Lamentation for J. Robert Oppenheimer
On the 70th anniversary of the dropping of the Atomic bomb on Hiroshima and Nagasaki, 1945-2015

At the Los Alamos visitor's center
his swivel chair is on display in a glass case,
its worn to the woodgrain arms
held up his raw thin elbows,
hunched over the chaotic heat of his war desk
with the dragon's breath
of General Groves on the back of his neck.
The threadbare flattened seat reeked
of something that lost its security clearance,
while his smoker's cough
wanders the ground zeros of eternity.

Last night the scientists danced to
sultan of swing Glenn Miller,
drank perfect manhattans,
drunk dialed Georgia O'Keeffe,
talked Fat Man's Gorgon-skulled nest
of hot scrambled wires,
had an irradiated venison feast,
those who couldn't drive
followed the red horse of the Apocalypse
into glowing Jacona arroyo.

After a night of twisting and sweating
in the sheets, he receives the first edition
of the Bhagavad Gita.
He rides to aspirate the world's grieving every night,
he rides to the smoking, burnt-out end of days.
He prefers to ride under a curfew of stars,
he knows that this maimed,
praying for rain desert is
hallowed ground,
is killing field,
is dream land
the space between poems.

The Spicer Variations

Poet Jack Spicer "does not like his life written down. He was born in Hollywood In 1925. Anyone interested in further information should contact him at THE PLACE, 1546 Grant Avenue, San Francisco."

–The New American Poetry, 1945-1960, Grove Press, 1960.

I don't believe in the Wizard of Oz or unidentified
flying objects. My heart is made of
whatever the moon is. Across the deadly
desert we found petrified shadow where the
poem lasts as long as human touch.
Signs of life are vivid and ghostly pale.
There is a long trail into the
back country, in this heat, choose your
victims carefully.

Around the campsite we argued over
how hot it has to get for the desert
to hold us in the fire of its fanged smile.

*

I've been praying to the broken gods for
rain for five days and for five days more.
I rise in the morning to see the
treacherous sun and try to cut for sign
on the pavement. Indians are everywhere
and no rain. In my dream last night

there were rain drops. They came in from
the west on the wind and softened
the treacherous blue. I've learned to
smell clouds that make rain. They drop
terror and guns, and hearts and skies
with holes in them. Indians show me the
tracks, they soften and grow old
in the heat. So do the tracks. I am one
imaginary elegy away from grace.

*

Frieda explains how her husband
D.H. Lawrence's ashes were once stolen
and later recovered. She met the thief in a
Taos bar, a San Cristobal neighbor, he gave
them up under the grave threat of castration.
The moon was round and full.
Frieda laughs at how she mixed his ashes
in with concrete and sand and how it became
a huge concrete slab. It would weigh over a ton.
New Mexico laid him down to sleep.
The Puebloans called her *Angry Winter*.
The blue sky is no longer treacherous and
is generous with Pueblo time.
D.H. owes Jack Spicer a decent living. The
desert sweats like a lover visiting
his high country crypt.

Coyote Journalist
-Charles Bowden 1945-2014

Follow his blood orchids
down night-blackened rivers
fed by endangered glaciers
into the Sierra Pinacates
of the world where extinct volcanoes
speak in occult tongues
past rattlesnakes bobbing and weaving
against blue sky
while the universe buzzes
with hidden constellations.
What's left of the still breathing river
bleeds into the Sea of Cortez
a shadow of its pristine source
its curvaceous meandering
once sustained generations traveling half-naked
across forbidden
dunes in the heat.

Respite from the drug mules, Juarez shape
changers, the lurid documentation of
young maquiladora women
lunches with sicarios and their
grave senses of self
was always the wild Sonoran hummers,

no strangers to war
that blitzed plastic nectar blossoms
like hell's angels
in your backyard of weary bliss.

Your beloved *desierto*
riotous with new life has
always been
may not always be
just the same as you left it.

Massacre
–for Joe Somoza

On any other Sunday if the kitchen
light had a voice it would sing
like Mavis Staples
all the birds would be
politely silenced by the poet
who sits in his
Las Cruces garden on mornings
like this for
twenty-two years
writing poems
in the shade of a tall tree
so he wouldn't later on lose his mind.

The rooster would crow dawn up
from polished black to soft blue
full-throated throughout the neighborhood
many of the children would go
politely and without incident to mass
my prayer flags would still have nine lives.
On any other Sunday,
nobody would rise haunted with the
ghost sickness
or deny the Coyote within.

Anybody would believe the full moon
or at least the ghost of moon
as yellow as yarrow
as it traveled across the shores of our eyes
or June with its rampaging fahrenheits.
Each tree is an indeterminate amount of
time rooted deep.
We think, therefore we think we're an act of faith
unfathomable morning
we're walking through cottonwood snow.

Paris Elegy #5

We roared with them in Paris
We were a million strong in our hearts
we broke ourselves against the vanishing
shore ice, against the desert noir under
our feet, against the soft raiments of lasting
love. They blasted us out of our saddles
for our satiric cartoons, the drifting passivity of
the Seine swelled with rivers of bloodied streets,
for every paint or word slinger turning over in his or her grave,
a Villon, some Rimbaud, some Picasso lying un-
deterred at heaven's gate, tried to broker the peace
with their spirits. Nobody would be cured, cursed or saved,
but the words will always flow into the undisturbed
pearlescence of the river. In the half-light
end of the day only the dead are praised for their
poise, we'll still scratch our words and images *vive le France!*
on the walls of every via dolorosa on earth where a
hemisphere of shadows dance and our offerings are made
whole by the indiscriminate quills of the sun.

Paris Elegy #6

The clerestory lets in the grey
November half-light,
the color of breaking heart
after breaking heart
on a Paris street in a murderous time.
Armed with Kalashnikovs, they slaughtered
Charlie Hebdo's editorial offices and
we wondered how shall the heart be re-
constituted after its feast of losses?

Time, an impossible companion, lifts the
words Proust left behind.
Lifts the bitter frozen bones of the dead
like death's collector, in disquieted dust dervishes
high above the living:
                      taking its walk of mayhem in the
breaking winter cold.

I have found a tribe for my aging devotions and it is dis-
oriented, scattered on four winds, I can see their
faces in the clerestory windows, along with those
who fell away before our eyes.
The skein of resistance that runs through us
must not unravel.

Back home, we asked the lost generation of candidates
would they've killed Hitler as an infant?
Would they have waterboarded Villon who was born
the year Joan of Arc was burned at the stake
national poetry month in the lowlife April city of Paris?
Is Jesus desperado enough to absorb on our behalf
the next suicide bomb blast?
In this our time
                our journey to the end of the night.

Elements of Mystery and Surprise

Nicanor Parra said, *take back everything I said*
anti-poetry was his game and he took it to his grave
his vernacular Chilean love fest with language
permeated my life with hard-edged oblivious
soul and a militant wonder at everything that moves,
that is beautiful or sorcerous, everything a surprise.

That he died at 104 in January is no surprise,
he took his wild white hair with him to his grave
and for a moment I thought of my mother's oblivious
end, and how silence is its own language
how it stalks and centers the mind, how it moves
through rooms on its own recognizance, left unsaid.

In poetry everything is permissible, or so he said.
You can't improve the blank page from the grave.
I've always been attracted to sorcerers of language,
who braved elements, watched winter's blind moves
without flinching, who used words that surprised,
romanced each with a knowing. Death to the oblivious.

Like those beautiful Chileans Bolaño and Neruda,
oblivious to the sorceries and machinations of fate, they
stalked language with the wild passion of martyred saints,
there ain't no grave worth its weight in silence that could
still the bold surprise of their words. Nothing unspoken,
everything left to be said:winter drives us deeper in, wind
takes a breath but still moves.

Across landscapes wretched with drought, the ancients move
with the alacrity of wind, each track, each bone is a surprise
and if we dig deep enough, the words appear in a language
we don't recognize but we do, where whispers of wind said:
everything permitted, nothing survives the ground, the
oblivious takes root. Even then the world seemed cruel,
its condition grave

its black ghost horses stared at ghost borders on ghost graves.
I visit my mother's grave and everything we said
is above the ground, in the wind, safe in the house oblivious
the passages of time. I think of her, of Nicanor, memory moves
us from one dimension to another. Every blank page a surprise.
Nicanor, your anti- is my anti-. Reminds me that snow is the

language of silence. Chile isn't Colorado, another language.
A kid in winter is waiting for the bus in the wind, it moves
to allow for the coming mysteries and the elements of surprise.

II

In Praise of Winter's Essentials

the force that words obey in song
the rose and artichoke obey
in their unfolding towards their form.

—Robert Duncan

Anthropocene

Like a single species in the Anthropocene dominates
all nature on the planet, I impose my will on this backyard.

Craven wildfires of California are hot enough to bend time.
I wonder how much wattage in a life is dimmed in the end

for failure to save the whales? A beached stillbirth is not
Kafkaesque. St. Anthony of Padua's hallucinations

are attributed to the ingested fungi found in rye bread,
the symptoms of ergotism influenced Northern Renaissance

painting. Once the fungi had one of its alkaloids distilled into
Lycergic Acid, the U.S. Army tried to impose its will on the

world. The cost of anti-venin for a rattlesnake bite equals the
time it takes to recite the Mourner's Kaddish 100 times.

Words like thoughts and prayers impose their will on nothing,
are inorganic, don't biodegrade, but they are flammable

and burn easier than flag-draped coffins. The bones of threatened
Right whales are buried at sea and after eons will come back

as fossilized starlight. Even this Apache plume with its fragile,
celestial blooms is as brittle as a crone, an evolutionary response

to the desert's search for rain. In 1945, Max Ernst painted *The Temptation of St. Anthony*, a surrealist's response to the

Holocaust. I take my pulse and can hear a Patti Smith song from *Horses*. Each one is wild and borderline shamanic. You can see

their breaths in winter from a thousand miles away. A few feet away a raven steals a food nugget from my dog's dish. He's

bounced up a ladder of willow branches before I can say go in peace. I wonder if his trickster instinct trumps my reverie of

self-absorption? Our dotages wait for us in unmarked cars with expired plates, will ask us if we trafficked in beauty,

if we were part of the problem, if our methods were unsound.

First Day of Autumn

I ground myself to the morning
and rediscover this
chain of perceptions   old man
raven his cottontail overkill prickly-
clawed carrion dance
    trickster saint of the
               arid blue

the leaves
      in scurrying coarse whispers
scour the land of its impurities, its compost,
the remnants of summer's immense
    dialogue with life
             measured in these disinterred
moments that won't
crumble in the hand.

Last of September's
           few and far between
flirtatious clouds
unburdened
cling to the sky.

Standing Rock

In the black earths of October
the precognizant will dance, no
timing no telling when or how this
might end. But it has an ending built
in. Just like October in North Dakota ends
far north of itself and delegates the snow.
In the old days they say you could monkey wrench a
dozer until it froze in place, a relic blushed
with rust, zoned deep into its paralysis. The ground
is well worn, the elixir of history just below the surface.
The oily smells of a wastrel's cash permeates
the clothing. Men in glass buildings fetishize its
order and flow, every resource its price. The
white-eye lawyers wear loud moccasins.
These cool evenings are consumed by smoke that's
hung here unabashedly for centuries. It is praised
and it is spoken. It lingers in the clothing of people
who'll be here long after it's over. The ashamed
fixated dogs strain at security leashes. Rez dogs
patrol the spark spitting campfires from the periphery.
The water, *the water* visible from space
deserves the immensity of its time unmolested underground.
Winter will come to this place, to all of us, in time
and too soon. It'll roar and howl over us like a white
blinding sea. In my mind there's the frozen locomotive
breaths of wild ponies and the delicate frost disappears
swiftly on the Cannonball's exposed stones. We're all
moving closer to the fire. The struggle is built in, we'll
reconnoiter spring for an ending that may not last.

Indian Summer

With a line by Robert Duncan

October is the existential comfort
of a fleece autumn sidewalk.
It stills in a drowsy, unkempt
garden kind of way,
a chattering Sunday fruit trees
and sparrows grazing kind of way.
Every enlightened yellow leaf that falls
at its serendipitous zenith like sheet music,
resurrects the soul of one priest
disappeared by cartel *sicarios* and
buried in a Mexican graveyard.
Resurrects Robert Duncan's shadow.
Resurrects the cave wall Blunderer kachina who
carries on an ongoing dialogue with Columbus Day.
Becomes the force *that words obey in song*.
To love October is to anthropomorphize
all the gods and fetishize none. To love
October is to obey the durability of time in living color.

In Praise of Winter's Essentials

Our old roadhouse
neglected once upon a time
years under the weather,
no Fallingwater
nor O'Keeffe's Black Place
this place we applied enough raw knuckles
and bent backs
until it made sense to
                    live in.

Heavy first snows of October
disappeared quickly on the ziggurats
of cordwood season after season
their lessons in muted presence.
We curried favor with the gods
of recycling.
Inside, her hands made of plaster felt for
nature's contours of stone and mud
each finished wall a blank canvas
another dimension to the warmth.
Reframed double-paned windows gave
new quiet clarity to the remains of the day.

Some years the land surrendered
to winter's empty grave of drought

some years the wind spoke only in
romance languages
some years the wind was a desert without borders
or the sky's vanquished whisper.

Soon I'll enter this home for
the last time, speak to it as if it's always
drawn its strength of breath
from the earth, its warmth says
you never really *own* a place

but sometimes it responded
to our touch.

Poem to My Younger Self

First, you recognize January 20th
the coldest day on record in hell.
You re-enter the U.S. at Organ Pipe,
carrying two smuggled litres of tequila,
and read Ginsberg's *The Fall of America*
to your half-gypsy girlfriend
with her fishnet stockings and
an *I'm with Her* ballcap as she drives
across the *despoblados*,
                        as quiet as virga,
towards Gila Bend before dark.

Where you once saw vertiginous
American beauty there will be black
blotches that remind you of Motherwell's
elegies to the Spanish Republic.
The saguaro night makes out its last
will and testament. You light another
candle and hope its liminal glow
guides you to its inventory of wonders.
Under a Christmas grey sky,
a black cat sits under a
bare tree and you herald it
as an omen. Like Yamabushi,
            you go off with her clear-eyed and
long-haired to sleep in the mountains.

Your true rhetorical sobriety
is years away yet you've
been ambushed by the world's
disequilibrium, you're
in danger of tipping over.
Am I better able to handle this
tsunami of political grief now than
when I was your age?
Which of us has more to lose?
I can't remember the last
time the world trafficked in grace.
Long gone are the days when visions
of sugarplums became images of
surly nuns and stigmatas,
my first wet kiss,
driving at night on acid,
     or early reconnoitering mad songs of
language.

Let's exchange texts.
I'll trade you my Hugo's graves and
rivers for your *Journey to the End of the Night*.
Even then, devout cynic, you felt the
flickering presence of future soul,
the powers that be gave you a chiaroscuro world.
The winter clouds are somber
December grey, I remember the slow
motion of your childhood.

Never stop showing your teeth to power.
This row of votive candles in the window
provides no warmth but
the light is gentle,
                projects verve and solidarity:

we flicker in and out of each other's lives.

Distance Over Snow

For Bob Anderson

One night you called long distance newly
arrived in Minnesota, a lonely voice
filled with faithful drunken purity
like a poem by Malcolm Lowry.

You disgorged the still warm truths
from our brotherly bones while giants
in the earth, year after year peel our
fingers off the grip we held on our boyhoods.

The solstice ice on the ponds outside
your Eden Prairie window is as thick
as sleep, but our memories, always thawing
break off into smaller, knowing pieces,

become more fluid, flowing, and in
your voice I equate smoke and whisky
with camaraderie. It is late, our voices
ache with frost, I can hear the distant coal trains

clatter east through snow, their destinations
obscured by spewed grime. The night sky
holds its discourse above the minutes it takes
for your words to slowly fade. I can hear your

bones aching like a scarecrow's, are tired with
the crossing of primitive Iowa's and full moon
Nebraska's. The lakes, mostly ice are Indian head
nickel- flat and silvery in distances too close to

the road to be of much use to the wits. I
imagine you clattering along in that apartment
after a hard day's work, scattering dishes, old
episodes of The Twilight Zone, calling old friends

from somewhere hear the dark side of James Wright's
Lake Minnewaska – you are alone, you share nothing
if not the north wolves secret name with the universe.
You are nothing if not full of an unsustainable peace,

I am nothing if not your friend. I set the receiver down
and can hear you crack open another cold one in a kitchen
1100 miles away while I draw a yellow map of our
old neighborhood in the snow.

Late April

A red tail hawk drifts
over North Cochetopa Pass
beneath a capricious spray
of summer-lit clouds.
Carries the squirming
change of seasons
in his claws.

Leaving Notes for the Underworld

Gazing out onto the garden from this sunburst kitchen
as if the earth-touching Buddha
left us totems of grace overnight
I want to believe each new hollyhock or sun-
flower ends a
small war somewhere.

There's a lone hummingbird at the feeder, one
of the universe's tiny drones of *presence*
hovering near my ear
brings news of a world hysterical from afar,
on a flight path no listless god could follow.

The day's usual aggressive
                              contrary beat
                                                   now softly dropped

into a regular pace

I throw on a pair of levi's, Hawaiian shirt
my cowboy boots, eleven minutes before work
on a sunny Berrigan sonnet kind of day, I salute the
ceramic Buddha on the kiva fireplace: *adios!* While
summer in so many words
touches the earth.

Lenitive

Last night, the heat between us reformed our motley bodies
into separate but equal parts. At 6:30 a.m. the first thing I hear
is jazz radio alarm doo-wop. I sit on the edge of the bed as the
crack of dawn creaks me awake. Some of my joints

rebel against the tribe and ache for the habañero balm of
the sun. I feel every stone I hoisted, every dog's grave I dug.
I brush all my teeth, make coffee. Read Ron Padgett:
a raunchy, terrifying God. I've always loved the New York

School. I've decided I'm a gangster without portfolio. I check
the weather over America and the negative capability of the
latest category four. August gave up its lush ghosts, roots and
songs. September has lifted the moratorium on simple acts

of mercy. Mimosa is just heaven spelled backwards, its blossoms
reveal the sun's inner light, which reveals an epiphanic gallery
of born morning soothsayers: canyon wren, Grace's warbler,
snowy owl —

the only raunchy, terrifying God is human and they feel our
radical warmth everywhere. How did you come to me to place
your wings of language between my lips? You burned your
meanings deep into open ground on blackened Sabbaths of

tribal desert crossings, you belonged to every struggle, no precipitation forecast. You burned through our voices hoarse with resistance through breath and memory, earth's oldest friend, denuded and deceased by noon, in a fierce dialogue with

the gloaming, and resurrected, a second coming, again every dawn. By your light the oldest drawing in the world was done with an ochre crayon. Your light is lenitive, our separate but equal parts ache to become one.

Burial Ground

She's burying our dog in the cicadian
heat of solstice. She idles over the
misshapen pile of grave rock, grieves
alone sitting on hallowed Apacheria.
Some day, dogs will return to the autocthonous
spirit of cave bear long before the
Aztec domesticated the tomato or Route
66 or *capulin* became Spanish for choke-
cherry, a word as tactile as a gypsy moth
on her tongue. Today, the staked plains rise
in the haze. She slaps some earth off her bare knees.
The wind blows us back into our
families in dusty summertime micro-
bursts of morning remembrance.
She had a favorite blanket. We wrap
her in the longest day of the year.

the old place

out here
a few of our ghost dogs
frolic beneath the prayer flags
on a hot
summer day
field of stone

ghosts of poems, too

in a dry heat's crackling solitude
they flutter about like every
bird I've
ever named
singing in the one tree
that grows in the collected
places of my mind.

Moon Song

Years ago the moon used to
follow me home
between Glorieta Pass
and Starvation Peak,
full of itself
as fragile as an eggshell
as inconsequential as the anonymous deceased son
of a Ukranian gangster –
behind its worn raw bright power
a pockmarked Yorick face glowed with a
cheap heavenly magic

my introverted friend preferred the
company of its vast blackened solitude to the
intimacy of complete strangers
abdicating nothing but the end
of the night.
It once rose over Hernandez
frozen in time
once feigned boredom from years
of glowering at me on earth
from space.

Thankful

Some mornings I wake up just thankful enough
for the unsaid things, the string of things better not left

estranged, for the anecdotal anarchy of this or that fate.
Stevie Ray Vaughn's hat. Frida Kahlo's enigmatic gravitas.

For not being haunted by rivers. For traveling in the dark
mistaken for nobody in particular, for sanctuary cities,

their nightly glow. For my casual acquaintance with pure,
blind luck. I once held a Gauguin Tahiti journal next to my

heart and could feel it tremble with new paradisial life.
I once flicked an Arizona vinegaroon off my sleeping bag.

I once rhapsodized how forest bathing really is a thing half
a world away. In the arctic, poet dg nanouk okpik's corpse whale

raven pecks indelicately at the supernova of half-rotten innards
strewn across the ice. I'm thankful for those who expose the

sexual predations of the powerful. For turkey vultures whose one
defense against predators is foul-smelling regurgitation. I once

gazed at the elaborate root system of the universe without
dropping an empty hummingbird's nest cradled in my hands.

Their absence no less mysterious than the breadth of evening sky.
The red splotch on a sand hill crane's head is the sun, I'm sure of it.

His feathers, the grey industrial snow. I could see him,
his legacy of stillness, from the cold road. For these clouds broken

into aboriginal languages, for the belabored silence of the river.

Universe of Poems and Dreams

I read poetry like there's no
yesterday. These improbable dreams are
like that, no yesterday, no tomorrow.
Conjurings that somehow have something to say

somewhere to be besides this endless
circumnavigating the luminous
universe. If, like poems,
they actually landed somewhere

they'd take on the truths of the terrain around them
would be more easily spotted by
drones, less easily bruised by
sullen archetypes, more tactile and responsive.

Dreams have the power to form their own cult,
a flotilla of other realms. Poems are left to
torch the heart and give voice
to its vast charcoal remains.

Lone Essentials

Distance over snow is simply that: harder to get there from here. The old neighborhood in a cooler time. Immaculate tawny lawns. Had to visit the desert to discover stars gave the rocks I collected their intransigent magic. My mother deep into her disease haunted the house while alive. There's no removal of even the subtlest tyrannies but sometimes the sun reveals the subtlest of reconciliations, even after burying the dead deep in the mind so close to home.

*

When I was younger I was an impoverished provocateur, kite flyer, Schwinn stingray rider king of my fate. It would take some time but I'd learn my life was no outlier. Distracted from my destiny by improvisation, I listened as John Coltrane reached for that lone essential that hung suspended forever at breath's end.   Tender, whispered things too, revealed sometimes the forgotten lyricism of dilated memory. When I was younger borders were horizontal rainbows. Every kind of blue dawn thrasher sang
free jazz!
free jazz!

*

She's devoted to its paradisial spirit, a country unto itself orioles empurpled nightshade   fastidious monarch flits from yarrow blossom to yarrow blossom. The artichoke and rose unfold toward their forms. Even during days of lost cause drought, even in the engorged rising phoenix of the heat: her essential pollinators, songs her mother taught her, whipping black snake soaker hoses in place, a ground cover of seeds for the mourning doves. It's easy to get lost in her white hot shadow. She basks in the presence of her persistent songbirds of now.   I look back at all of our July evenings indentured to the idea of each other, our paradisial spirits of resistance joined at the heartbeat sheltered by the glow of night sky's far country.

III

Gorge Songs

A provocative sorcerer is the gorge.

—John Nichols

poem/river

Imbiber of oblivious moon beams,
chaser of uncharted space to unspeakable places,
trailblazing book of origins
before original sin
fractured gorge digger in the Van Gogh light of spring
proselytizer of gneiss
and schist, long-
              bodied muse of curvaceous
erosions
      wild RIVER!

I deliberate on your impatience as you pass by,
taking all track of time and leaving it
behind. Poem is the self that flows
through you, you erode the soul's grievances
until you reach bedrock.

Fell asleep one night next to the Rio Grande
and woke up to canyon wren's skitter over white
water like false eyelashes flirting with the gods.
Woke up to

              Crow flying crying crow flying cold
to
   lyrical white noise google earth wave
below gentle flock formations breaking up and
reconstituting over the endless river less
traveled
      POEM

The River's End

Bleached out moon in blue sky
high noon possesses the Zen of a snowflake.
The river is a chain that links the lost spaces in
the desert between stars. The stars

are like the remains of any anonymous poet's
bones that suddenly wash up on shore
somewhere in Mexico. In Palo Duro Canyon
ghost Kiowa follow a Cooper's hawk to a

dry stinking spring. At the museum,
Shakespeare's first folio is on display and open
to a page from Hamlet: *unpack my heart with words.*
It's Valentine's Day Sunday, the world is trying

its best to love me. Unpack these words and
underneath in the circumspect late light of day, the
lissome river gathers up the heartbreak, the beauty,
its altar boys, spider's webs, snake rattles, politicians'

barbaric kitsch, the face of Buddha and deposits them
on some far shore of my mind where there is still
elasticity and order, no war.
A dusky peace settles over the land

just as the river defuses its long, hot summer and
flows slow on the earth into autumn.

The Day They Polluted the Animas

my voice rusted shut
the defoliant sun burned a hole in
all the fevered characters of my being.   Raven
feathers dropped like leaflets on Tokyo before the
fire bombing.   Nobody

takes first do no harm for granted and then gives it back.

Can't see the blood moon rising through the
legions of flies, the thick aromas of dark industry
the unholy hues of once pure roaring waters.

Coal ash waste in South Carolina creates its own
    stygian canals struggling to breathe,
they run without sense or direction,
    an apocalypse mascara.
In aerial photos flowing bauxite waste is a deranged
    watercolor landscape run amok,
plumes of toxic foam flow into a magenta river
    as if the earth had been nuked from orbit.
Molten sulfur is a rivulet of bright blood from
    a razor thin incision at the tar sands refinery.

What is underneath the surface is what
is worth knowing in our souls. The
Indians worry that without the river their
languages will become dead things

    remembered only when sifting through ash.

Gorge Song

For Tony Moffeit

Two men from Taos Pueblo
watch a mountain
bluebird pull the remains of the night
with her into the introverted first
light of the gorge.
She was all
that moved across the volcanic field.
Its petrified blackness shimmered
at daybreak
without the aegis of a single
human trespass.   They
heard the laughter from deep
in the sage, they heard
coyotes gone crazy for a junk moon
they heard the drumming of the
stars disappear in the snow.
They heard the echoes
inebriated with song.

St. Patrick's Day
for Jane

We yearn to be taken away too
while watching the delicate remains of
family turn for home, consumed on their way
by the interior reaches of the snow brightened canyon.
It was that kind of deep overcast day,
to pray to Ogma, to Brigit, to scrawl their
names in river sand, to fall away once more
from the voices of blood kin
floating in fresh memory like lucky charms.
Riding the rapids I learn to be taken away,
to obey the instinct that says:

you can't follow
that says from high in the sky:
you make your own fire.

The friction of distances creates the
smallest of flames to burn their names
into the river with, watch it take them away,
hear it sizzle as they leave. Without that there
is no turning for home
only the shadows of the canyon and the
frantic whispers of white water flowing
over stone, saying nothing still.

Rio Grande Gorge: in memorium

We're hiking across the waist-high grey
sage of the rim,
seven thousand feet
the hull of the cloud is pink hardened
fire. I swallow mouthfuls of dry wind.
It rises from the gorge
a shapeless force of invisible horses,
a breath from the middle
of the earth.

To get my bearings, I have to leave off large
portions of memory and bring others
back alive. Amidst the stone-spawned shadows
on river's surface lie the thousand voices
of the unruly fallen: each
                              of them a storyteller, a
stray tall tale, a strict truth, a confession
unburdened.

I plunge my hand into the feral icy waters
of the Rio Grande.
The current is big-hearted and listens to the voices
then and now, of no return, once here
and vehement with extinguished grace, now
downstream, somewhere faraway,

into thin air.

Turning for Home

Wingbeats that've become so much my heart's
rhythm, we've been permitted
this wild walk,
those blackened witchy whooshes
in the empty overhead,
the gorge an abyssal slice of heaven.
Name-drop words like vertigo, *esperanza*,
breathless and forgotten,
the ravens will leave them like scar
tissue in the sage. Turning for home
for them is a
slow climb into an icy sea
of spirit bear clouds.
Turning for home for me is gathering
her close against the wind,
finishing the trail mix,
hiking back into exiled boulevards, our
estranged small worlds,
less spirited realms.

The River

That autumn night's coyotes' distance-
defying cries, their eerie lyricism,
soundtrack to the barely visible, echoes
embedded deep in the cataracts below.
Follow them to the source: a roar of white noise
from the beginnings of borrowed time.

Makes most wakened nights inhabitable,
washes the dying light of the first camp fires
into the future's opaque here and now.
In the riverine hot springs
I feel the shedding of this deadened skin,
dream a dream before it succumbs to total abstraction.

    Some nights, I feel bereft, estranged,
as much a part of humanity as I am
                  Saturn's rings.

Follow the thieves of time in out of the cold
from under a night sky so vast the imagination couldn't
possibly embellish the river any more so
than that. Follow the reflection of
the full moon's crossing, it quivers on the
fierce black water's surface.

At the same moment, in Chile,
in the Atacama, it shines on the first inch
of rain in years, the desert floor covered with a
dream carpet of pink mallow.
Its dry Capiapo River whispers to the Rio Grande:

Feel blessed,
        here is where water comes to die.

Remembered moments when a river carried me through
resolute darkness, allowed love to surface, take root,
gave the intoxicating discovery of it room to breathe,
its inscrutable spirit offered openly.
The loss of river words given zombie life in the
darkened cavity of the cañon:

  her beauty is territorial
in time
she made me believe
this is where we began.

Robert Creeley in Taos

    Robert Creeley
never comfortable with Indians, greetings
across
        the arroyo, how far across time and space
the distance between people   gets into
a bar fight during fiesta,
can feel his eye breaking
gazes helpless and merciless into the
winter gorge's void.

The distance between the bridge and
its blue river below delivers another world
to him,
is a suicide room,
an airy of light and silence
an otherworldly reimagining of space
where the blood moon's shine rests
the havoc of the world in place –

always talking,
he shouts *drive, he said*
and the echoes return
in the remote thin air

look out where yr going

September

Cooler by a degree or two, awake in the softened
darkness, the sun a vague hue behind
mountains without shape
like the first words in my head
unburdened by meaning or form
one gradually attracting another
the first things that come to mind are these

insomniac elders
indispensable and restless
                                       a rosary of
mourning doves assemble in a summering
queue, balanced, high above the river.

First light is like a venerated saint, nebulous
dream-state fevered glow of moment,
listen to the cañon echo with the dove's
plaintive song,
feel in the words
the vibration of buried time.

Solstice River Poem

A *descanso* marks the place where a highway
fatality happened. One boy was killed
instantly, another, witnesses say,
walked off into the night unharmed, never
to be seen again.
      He disappeared in the dead of winter.

People are really from this place.
Their blood passes through the ground
so deep their spirits can't
be seen out walking
      in the cold.
  Nobody is
as old as they once were
recollected by the light of December stars.

So far, my next breath has not been alone
and is visible again. The territory beyond the moon
is desert and the river is
sullen with forgotten winters.
This is where those remaining remember to
honor their own darkness and
this land with all its inviolable anarchies
    drifts that much closer
  to faint sun.

Christmas at Picuris Pueblo

Pungent cedar smoke
clings to our eyelashes
tough humpbacked darkened hills of
morning wrapped close around each
of us
you could feel the great earth intelligence,
this disheveled hour in the
sweet irrevocability of time
no permit required.

Remains of last night's
bonfires in still smoking
charcoal splotches gave me the
feeling of deliverance
of no more velocity
than standing
beneath white moon
near the Matachine dancers in street clothes,
devil clown in a Santa hat cracks a whip,
thirty of us standing in the Sangre de
Cristos wind chill
on holy ground
on bone songs
or forgotten starlight long
buried with the ashes and
        the spirit of
                heavenly peace.

solstice walking poem

    the morning sky all over
us, sunrise a still life's blood
orange in the mind's eye
we must be in the range
of everything:

    somebody once said beauty is being able
to transmit
an otherworldly truth
: the discovery of thirty percent
more matter in the universe
with its new inventory of light

    these four
bluebirds shifting their weight
the cold wind
ruffling feathers
on a wire fence.

NOTES

Border Wall Blues

"commensurate with my capacity of wonder."
F. Scott Fitzgerald, The Great Gatsby,
narcocorridos Mexican folk songs celebrating
the illegal drug trade

Incident at Tinaja del Indio

tinaja Spanish for seasonal rock water
tank or small reservoir,
ahimsa: The principal of non-violence towards
every living thing

At the Anasazi Winery

Sherwin Bitsui: Diné poet from Arizona, excerpt from
Flood Song, Copyright, 2009 by Sherwin Bitsui. Reprinted
with the permission of The Permissions Company, Inc. on
behalf of Copper Canyon Press, www.coppercanyonpress.org

Birds

Takes place within the Bosque del Apache Wildlife Refuge,
near Socorro, New Mexico.

"birds are poems I haven't caught yet" Jim Harrison, excerpt
from the poem "The Tiny Bird", from *Dead Man's Float.*
Copyright 2016 by Jim Harrison. Reprinted with the
permission of The Permissions Company, Inc. on behalf of
Copper Canyon Press, www.coppercanyonpress.com

Saguaro

Mark Klett: noted Southwest landscape photographer
James Wright: Minnesota poet.

Gila

"there is no hardship . . ." Ghassan Zaqtan, from the poem "Only Her Dream Will Tell of Her", from *Like a Straw Bird, It Follows Me & Other Poems,* Yale Univ. Press, 2012.

Winter Poem

John Weiners: noted San Francisco and Boston poet, author of the Hotel Wentley Poems.

"the wind is in charge of lives tonight."

Poet Bob Kaufman, from the poem "Images of Wind", from *Solitudes Crowded with Loneliness,* New Directions, 1965

To My Mother

"the devil's ass blackened by smoke", a variation on a line by the Marquis de Sade.

Aeolian

Giving forth or marked by a moaning or sighing sound or musical tone produced by or as if by the wind

Lamentation for J. Robert Oppenheimer

"Sultans of Swing" a pop song by the band, Dire Straits "Good Morning, Aztlán", is the 10th studio album by the American band, Los Lobos. Aztlán is the legendary, original home of the Aztec/Mexican people.

The Spicer Variations

Jack Spicer was an influential West Coast poet who died of alcoholism at age 40 in 1965. Some of the anarchy and much of the spirit of this poem are influenced by several of his works.

Coyote Journalist

Charles Bowden was a famed border journalist, author of over 15 books and champion of the Mexican immigrant and those disappeared by cartel violence.

sicarios: Assassins.

Anthropocene

There are several forms of the Kaddish prayer recited at different times during religious services. This one is reserved specifically for mourners, and is recited daily for 11 months after a parent's death, then annually on the anniversary of the parent's death on the Hebrew calendar.

Standing Rock

The Standing Rock Indian Reservation is located in North Dakota and South Dakota in the U.S., and is occupied by ethnic Hunkpapa Lakota, Sihasapa Lakota and Yanktonai Dakota. It is located near the confluence of the Cannonball and Missouri rivers.

Indian Summer

"Blunderer kachina" hehe'a, one of the Zuni clown kachinas. "the force that words obey in song" by Robert Duncan, from the poem "Yes, As a Look Springs to its Face", from *The Opening of the Field,* Grove Press, 1960.

In Praise of Winter's Essentials

"Fallingwater" or the Kaufmann residence is a house designed by architect Frank Lloyd Wright in 1935, in rural Pennsylvania, 43 miles southeast of Pittsburgh.

"O'Keeffe's Black Place" Geographical area in New Mexico artist Georgia O'Keeffe painted to great acclaim.

Poem to my Younger Self

"Hugo's graves and rivers . . ." refers to some of Montana poet Richard Hugo's concerns.

Yamabushi: a Japanese ascetic hermit.

Late April

North Cochetopa Pass is in west-central Colorado.

Leaving Notes for the Underworld

"The day's usual, aggressive..." poet Ted Berrigan from the poem "Peace", from *Collected Poems of Ted Berrigan*, Univ. of California, 2005.

Turning for Home

esperanza: Spanish for hope.

Award- winning poet/playwright/essayist John Macker lives in Santa Fe, NM. His latest books are *The Blues Drink Your Dreams Away Selected Poems 1983-2018* (Stubborn Mule Press), *Gorge Songs* (DCArt Press,2017) with Denver woodblock artist Leon Loughridge and *Blood in the Mix* (with El Paso poet Lawrence Welsh) Lummox Press, 2015. In 2014 *Disassembled Badlands* was published (the 3rd book in the *Badlands* trilogy). Other books include *Woman of the Disturbed Earth, Underground Sky, Adventures in the Gun Trade , Las Montañas de Santa Fe* and *The Royal Road: Impressions of El Camino Real* (both in limited edition and with woodblock art by Leon Loughridge.). In 2006, he edited the *Desert Shovel Review*. He has won a Colorado Council on the Arts grant, A Colorado Arts (Tombstone) Award for Poetry and the 2006 Mad Blood magazine award for the long poem, "Wyoming Arcane."

www.ingramcontent.com/pod-product-compliance
Lightning Source LLC
Chambersburg PA
CBHW030121100526
44591CB00009B/486